AF619402

# 11 STEPS
# TO ARCHITECTURAL
# THESIS

ARCHITECT PROFESSOR
**INDRANIL SEN**

INDIA • SINGAPORE • MALAYSIA

ARCHITECT PROFESSOR

# INDRANIL SEN

**MUSIC**

**is the**

**Sonic Expression of**

**Harmony**

**Rhythm**

**Unity**

**And**

**Variety**

**So also is**

**ARCHITECTURE**

Contact Information
M: +91 98313 85880/ +91 84207 21201
E: IndranilSen.Net@GMail.Com
Website : www.arindranilsen.in

*Dedicated to my Brother-in Law*

*Asoke Chakraborty*

# CONTENTS

# FOREWORD

PROFESSOR
**DEVI PROSAD MALLIK**
**ARCHITECT ■ URBAN DESIGNER**
B Arch (CU); DTRP (CU); M Arch (UBC, Canada)

2A CHAKRABERIA LANE : FLAT NO. 202 (2nd Floor) : KOLKATA 700 020
■ TEL : +91 33 2486 4606 ■ CELL : +91 98301 09689 ■ E MAIL : dvpmallik@gmail.com

Dated : 28 November 2018

**FOREWORD**

It is indeed a great pleasure for me to respond to the request of Architect Indranil Sen to write the Foreword for his new book called 'Eleven Steps to Architectural Thesis'.

Architect Indranil Sen, has been a student of mine during his B. Arch Degree course in Bengal Engineering College, Sibpur (erstwhile BESU and now known as IIEST) and had been very diligent all the time. I still remember, as Professor and his Thesis Guide way back in 1980, his deep involvement and eagerness to excel in the field of Architecture. After Graduation, he has worked in many leading Consulting Firms, both in India and aboard and always feels proud of his body of work in the field of Architecture.

The purpose of this book is to appraise all final Year Students of Architecture, the various aspects of this exercise, called Architectural Thesis, and act as a reference, before commencement of the same.

This invaluable book is a mine of information, demonstrating all the stages of work that a Student Architect must go through for successful completion of his/her Thesis.

As there are not many books on such a subject for reference by students, this book, I am sure would be a very useful reference to all aspiring Architects and should be a storehouse of information.

The way this book has detailed out the steps to be followed for the final milestone, that is, the Architectural Thesis, is incredible. Going through this magnificent volume, I am amazed at the information and knowledge he has shared out of his international exposure.

In short, this book is unique and surely be a work to treasure for every Library of Schools of Architecture, as it categorically records all the activities and events that must be undertaken for this final lap of the B. Arch. Curriculum.

Wish him all the success

**Prof. Devi Prosad Mallik**
*Retd. Chief Architect (Acting), Dev. & Planning (T&CP), Govt of West Bengal*

*Professor – Design Chair: RR College of Architecture: SETGOI: Durgapur: West Bengal*
*Hony. Jury Member: Om Dayal College of Architecture*
*Visiting Faculty: JIS College of Engineering*
*Hony. Jury Member: UPSC Recruitment Board*
*Visiting Faculty: Guwahati College of Architecture*
*Ex Visiting Faculty: Piloo Modi College of Architecture, Cuttack*
*Guest Faculty & Examiner: BIT Mesra, Ranchi*
*Guest Lecturer & Jury: IIT Kharagpur*
*Ex Visiting Faculty: Jadavpur University*
*Ex Asst Prof: Bengal Engineering College, Sibpur*

# INTRODUCTION OF THE AUTHOR

Indranil Sen was born in Kolkata and is a graduate Architect from Bengal Engineering College, Sibpur, (erstwhile BESU and now IIEST) of 1980 batch and has always been a very serious professional.

In the last glorious 38 years of his career, he has worked in senior positions with leading Architectural and Developer organizations. Footprints of his project exposure are spread in 8 countries which include Oman, Mauritius, and Bangladesh to name a few.

He has also worked in projects in all the metros of India and in about twelve state capitals.

He has also acted as External Jury on invitation from IIT Kharagpur, Dep't of Architecture for assessing the final Year Project Dissertation and conducting Viva-voce Examination for their B. Arch Degree Thesis Program.

He has travelled extensively nationally and internationally and during this time, has worked on several prestigious projects with well known Architects & Engineers.

Presently he is a practicing architect in Kolkata and is the Principal Architect in Interface Design Studio, a firm jointly owned with his architect wife.

He has been associated with Academics and is an Ex-Visiting faculty in the School of Architecture, Techno India University, Kolkata.

He is also a Resource Person to the Council of Architecture, New Delhi, the apex body for Architects practicing in India.

**Contact Information**

Mobile : +91 98313 85880

E mail: indranilsen.net@gmail.com

Website : www.arindranilsen.in

**Other Books of the Author**

1. Theory of Architecture: Concept to Commissioning
2. Introduction to Architecture
3. Vaastu Saastra : Science NOT Ritualism

# PREFACE

Architectural Thesis or Dissertation, as may be called in some Schools of Architecture is one of the most important milestones for a student of Architecture. In India, as per the norms of the Council of Architecture and its recommended Minimum Standards of Architectural Education, "This is culmination of undergraduate studies and hence shall display the capability of the candidate to conceive/ formulate a design project and provide solution, aptly demonstrated through supporting research. The main areas of study and research can include advanced architectural design, including contemporary design processes, urban design including urban infill, environmental design, conservation and heritage precincts, housing etc. However, the specific thrust should be architectural design of built environment. Preparation of presentation drawings, working drawings, detailed drawings and study model are part of the requirements for submission. Submission of the Architectural Design Thesis Project shall be in the form of drawings, project report, models, slides, CDs and reports."

This book tries to document a process for students, so that they are aware of what are the do's and don'ts of this mammoth exercise called Architectural Thesis.

The book emphasizes on the process that may be followed to finally deliver a Project Design that truly reflects the capability and acquired confidence of a would-be Architect, before he jumps into the profession.

Congratulations and Best of Luck to all.

# ACKNOWLEDGEMENTS

Writing an acknowledgement for a book is never an easy task. The risk of unintentional omittance is great and thus would like to thank all the teachers of my life. I was fortunate to have some great teachers in school and college and would like to thank them all for making me, what I am today.

I am specially thankful to Professor Devi Prasad Mallik, my Thesis Guide during my B. Arch Program, who has kindly consented to write the Foreword of this book. Thank you so much Sir, for being one of the early lights in my career.

I would also like to thank all my friends and colleagues, from whom I have learnt what is written in the book. These are just documentations of those small but important facts on this subject.

I would have never written this book or any book, if I did not get a chance to share my knowledge with the students of School of Architecture, Techno India University. As a visiting faculty, I always found that there are very few points of reference on the basics of this subject and this thought had always made me feel that something needs to be done to assimilate this scattered information about this great subject so that there is no room left for any ambiguity or misconceptions.

Finally, a big 'thank you' to my family for sparing me the hours of time I spent on writing this book and sometimes at their cost.

**Indranil Sen**

*This book compares the entire chain of events, from inception to finish, to successful staging of a show*

*"ALL THE WORLD'S A STAGE"*

# STEP 1: INITIATION

THEME IT

AND

GET STARTED

# STEP 1: THEME IT AND GET STARTED

## 1.0 INTIATION

1.1 Understanding Architectural Thesis

1.2 Broad Shortlist of Project Type

1.3 Do not Repeat

1.4 Choose a Topic of your Dream

1.5 Never choose Specialized Projects

1.6 Check for Live project underway

1.7 Finalizing the Topic

1.8 Schedule of Activity

## 1.0 INTIATION

Hello everyone, specially, my Student Readers. This book tries to make your life a bit easier and inform you as to how to carry forward the huge submission called Architectural Thesis. As this is a Semester long exercise, many seem to lose their way midway, sometimes leading to a disaster. So getting ready is important as the whistle has been blown and the race for reaching the end has started.

### 1.1 Understanding Architectural Thesis

What is Architectural Thesis? In many Institute or Universities, this may be called Architectural Dissertation.

This is one of the most important milestones in the Under Graduate Architecture Education in India. This is perhaps the final lap of the journey and the last chance or window to showcase ones talent in this widely discussed creative Art with huge overtones of Science.

Architectural Thesis involves a process of designing a full sized project, which spans for a time period of about 4 to 6 months. There is much confusion in the minds of some as to why it is called Thesis. My understanding of this is that since the amount of work and the depth to which the study is involved, is so intense in nature, including doing some research work, many would compare this exercise to that of a Thesis, which is more often submitted for a Doctoral Program or Degree in other subjects.

Architectural Thesis is somewhat like a passport to the real life professional world along with the Bachelor's Degree. While the Degree is only proof ones academic proficiency, the Thesis Project work is the only proof of one's proficiency and efficiency as an Architect, and the level of understanding and expanse of creativity that one has acquired during the tenure of education in the School of Architecture.

The Final product is then evaluated by a team of expert, who are mostly Architects of repute from the professional world and Academicians. This is often called the *Grand Jury,* and is one of the biggest events in the entire Architectural Education Calendar every year.

## 1.2 Broad Shortlist of Project Type

To begin the process of this very important exercise, it is important to understand what kind of project types one is comfortable with. Most Institutes and Jury Members prefer and encourage students to choose live projects.

The primary idea is to find ones liking for a genre of architecture, like in music, every individual has a liking for a particular genre of music over some other genre. By similar analogy, every student of Architecture develops a liking for a particular type of project, where one feels comfortable or may be, has an ultimate dream to design a type of project.

I have thus always maintained and have said that-

> *"M U S I C is the Sonic Expression of*
> *Harmony, Rhythm, Unity & Variety*
> *So also is A R C H I T E C T U R E"*

Taking forward the analogy, this is like performing live on stage. A good and prepared musician always has a shortlist of numbers that he or she would like to perform. On stage, imaging him being told that there is time for only one number or song or recital; what would the musician do? He would choose the one number he is most comfortable with.

On the same lines, one must choose the Project Topic for Architectural Thesis in which he is most comfortable and confident.

The shortlist thus should be of projects of the genre that satisfies the above criterion.

## 1.3 Do not Repeat

Everyone one would say that a project topic should not be repeated. Do not choose any topic that has been dealt with during the last few Academic Years in the same Institute. It is also advised not to repeat project topics of nearby Institutes also as the Jury may be aware of this and comparisons are bound to happen. Thought of plagiarism may also arise if similar subjects are chosen. This is a very dicey position and one may take help from Teachers and Professionals to understand what would be the best choice. But one thing must be remembered; your Guide or Teachers will not tell you what to do unless you know exactly whay needs to be done.

## 1.4 Choose a Topic of your Dream

Many a times, you must have felt that, if I could design this building or that building that has been recently become famous. Or for that matter, a thought may have cropped saying if I had a chance to design that building, I would have done it this way.

Hurray, you may have got what you needed. Your Thesis/Dissertation Topic. Think over it. Let it grow on you for some time. Culture the topic and give time to get it to your nerves for some.

Let it become your only thought for a couple of weeks. As they say; eat, drink & sleep over the topic. Very soon your thoughts would take you to a dreamland, where the ideas will come flooding. Drown yourself in the thoughts that come and soak up all the useful and useless thoughts.

List them out. Try to find out the one avenue closest to your heart. Prepare the shortlist along with a synopsis.

Discuss with your Guide and others who you think would be your support system in the preparation of your project work.

Please remember also to talk to seniors of your institute and take help from them in narrowing down your Topic. First shortlist 5 topics, and then bring it down to three. Weigh all options, pros and cons of each of the topics, contemporary relevance. After taking into consideration all the facts and figures, ease of getting data related to the topic, choose your topic.

## 1.5 Never choose Specialized Projects

One must remember that the Architectural Thesis/ Dissertation is to exhibit to the Jury your proficiency in Architecture. Thus projects related to Urban Design, Town or City Planning,

Conservation etc. should never be chosen as they may be rejected for Architecture Thesis

It is also suggested that Area Development Projects, or large projects with many building and Master Planning needs should never be chosen. The risk in such topics is that the Jury finds it difficult to adjudge your caliber as an Architect and as result, your performance in the Grand Jury may end in disaster.

Similarly, topics with high end specialization requirements, such as, Conservation of Heritage Structures or Monuments, Interior Design Projects, Marine Architecture, should also be avoided. These topics may be of your liking, but are never suitable for the purpose.

### 1.6 Check for Live project underway

Your Dissertation Topic or Thesis Topic, as is called in many Institutes and Colleges or Schools of Architecture is very important. As has been explained earlier, choosing a live ongoing or proposed project topic helps in many ways. It is always easier to collect information for projects that are real. Keep your eyes open from the end of 8$^{th}$ Semester or 4$^{th}$ year and be on the hunt for your Thesis topic. As has been suggested before, make a shortlist and then proceed to finalize one topic you feel most comfortable with.

## 1.7 Finalizing the Topic

Make yourself a schedule. Allow a time windows for each activity and by the end of this first step, the Project topic must be chosen. Look for references and availability of information. It must also be remembered that your topic may not be absolutely original. Similar projects may have been taken up by earlier batches, but that should not deter you from choosing a similar topic. Here it is worth mentioning that similar is the word being used by me. Thus Cut and Paste topics should be absolutely avoided and is a big No.

Considering all the of the above, select your topic and then start your dream run.

## 1.8 Schedule of Activity

As may be understood, preparing an Activity Schedule is very important, depending on the time available in weeks. Fix a milestone that you need to achieve by the end of the given week. Here as word of caution, leave the last week free for doing all the fine tuning. Your entire submission should be ready by the penultimate week.

The Activities that are to be listed are the Chapter heads of this book.

A sample Activity schedule assuming that the entire exercise will be carried out in one full semester, that is 27 weeks is given below. The times allotted are generic and may be adjusted depending on the Thesis Topic and opinion of the Thesis Guide and Institute Faculties.

The Activity heads may be changed or altered or some additional heads may be added, as per requirements of a particular Thesis Topic. Also if the over time allotted by any Institute is less than 27 weeks, the Schedule would have to be altered to suit the reduced time.

An overall float of 2 weeks has been kept, just in case there is any un-comprehended delay.

***"The Secret Science of Architecture***

***is knowing the Art".***

## SAMPLE ACTIVITY SCHEDULE

***1 – Initiation***

1 week - from zero date to week 1

***2 – Thesis Guide Selection***

1 week - from end of week 1 to week 2

***3 – Collection & Collation of Info***

3 weeks - from end of week 2 to week 5

***4 – Design Inception (overlapped with above)***

5 weeks - from end of week 4 to week 9

***5 – Preliminary Design***

6 weeks - from end of week 9 to week 15

***6 – Schematic Design***

4 weeks - from end of week 15 to week 19

***7 – Draft Output & mock Presentation***

1 week - from end of week 19 to week 20

***8 – Project Report (overlap with earlier activity)***

6 weeks - from end of week 14 to week 20

***9 – Final Presentation***

2 weeks - from end of week 20 to week 22

***Physical Model (overlap with above)***

4 weeks - from end of week 20 to week 24

***10 – Getting Ready***

2 weeks - from end of week 22 to week 24

***11 – The Final Show***

1 week - from end of week 24 to week 25

# STEP 2: THESIS GUIDE

DIRECTOR PLEASE

# STEP 2: DIRECTORS PLEASE

**2.0 THESIS GUIDE**

2.1 Freeze Project Topic

2.2 Advice from Industry Professionals

2.3 Advice from Academics

2.4 Advice from Institute Faculty

2.5 Advice from Specialists or Mentor

2.6 Final advice from Guide

2.7 Reframe Project Brief

# 2.0 THESIS GUIDE

## 2.1 Freeze Project Topic

Once the Project Topic is finalized, have a heart to heart discussion with your Project Guide. He may have a few suggestions. Hear them out and then do the necessary tweaking in the Project definition. Kindly remember that such minor changes will keep on happening during the pendency of the preparation works. Do not get upset or agitated. Reason it out, if necessary with your guide and be convinced of the changes or modifications being suggested by him. Do not toe his line blindly.

## 2.2 Advice from Industry Professionals

Once the Project Parameters are more or less finalized, you may discuss them with Industry Seniors and Professionals. Here you Training contacts will be of much help. In this, you may discuss the entire project parameters with Architects, who may have done similar projects in real life.

Take all the first hand information available and stack them. You may not know, how some little information, which you now think is unimportant may turn out to be a face saver one day.

## 2.3 Advice from Academics

If you are lucky and have the ability to contact Teachers or Academicians from other Institutes, go and meet them. Reassure yourself that you are on the right track and your thinking is captured properly. There is no harm in exploiting the possibility of taking advice from knowledgeable Teachers and take valuable and important tips from them

## 2.4 Advice from Institute Faculty

Do not limit your interactions with your Thesis/Dissertation Guide only. Talk to other Faculty members also. Take their help. But one must remember a very important fact of advice taking. You need to have the ability to use the advice correctly and the ones that are relevant. Sometimes, an advice given by someone may not be useful to you. But still take note of it and stack it.

## 2.5 Advice from Specialists or Mentor

Your Thesis/Dissertation Project Topic may involve specialist inputs. Like for example, if you are planning to have Hospital or similar topic, you may think of taking inputs from Health Facility Planners who may not be architects. Similarly, specialized inputs form relevant discipline specialists may be taken.

It may also happen that you are fortunate to have a person who may agree to mentor you. Talk to him and take his advice.

## 2.6 Final advice from Guide

After all the inputs and information's received from the various sources, analyze and assimilate them. Having done this exercise diligently, discuss in detail with your Thesis Guide. Please allow him to give the final piece of advice. If there are contradiction in your thoughts or confusions on any matter, discuss with an open mind with your Guide and take his advice.

Like a game of Football, your Guide is the coach and you are the Player. He will be able to tell you what to do, but the ultimate playing has to be done by you, and execute the thought with your skill and imagination mixed with creativity. Your Guide may give you the first push, but the rest of the cruising has to be taken up by you.

## 2.7 Reframe Project Brief

Based on the advice received from your Guide, Mentor, Specialists of the Industry and other well wishers, reframe the entire Project Brief. This however may not be the Final Brief, but is the one you which will be your starting Block to start your Design Work. Start it with all the honesty. Never give up. Also remember that good designs come from good human beings. Thus, think with a lot of positivity.

***"You cannot Teach what you... do not Know***

***You cannot Preach what you... do not follow***

***You cannot Lead where you... cannot Go".***

# STEP 3: COLLECTION & COLLATION OF INFORMATION

SHOP FOR YOUR DATA

# STEP 3: SHOP FOR YOUR DATA

## 3.0 COLLECTION AND COLLATION OF INFORMATION

3.1 Data Collection

3.2 Development Control Rules

3.3 Zoning & Planning Guidelines

3.4 Info on available Site services

3.5 Old References

3.6 Site Information

3.7 Site Connectivity Data

3.8 Site Topography

3.9 Site Photos

3.10 Reference Images

3.11 Any other Relevant Info

3.12 Local Climatic Conditions

3.13 Potential Study

3.14 Analysis of all collected information

3.15 Site Analysis & Topography Study

3.16 Synthesis

## 3.0 COLLECTION & COLLATION OF INFORMATION

This step involves 3 important parts which will guide you to the true path leading to the destination. It will help understanding the project and its fine prints better. So proper and effective Collection, followed by Analysis and Synthesis and finally arriving at an Inference is the main goal, This exercise if done properly should act as an engine to drive the project to its logical conclusion.

Sometimes, data collection is good and full, but the final Inference is out of target. It is here that you must take the help of your Guide/Mentor, so that the next few steps are on the right path.

### 3.1 Data Collection

Congratulations.

You have just crossed the first large step which is also the most important step. Do not look back. You have chosen your topic after a lot of deliberation and consideration, and looking back will only make you sad, make you lose your confidence and a lot of valuable time that you have invested for the last couple of weeks or may be months will be wasted.

Jump to the next step. Start collecting all the data including Project Brief from the source that you believe in. Here it must be remembered that collection of good and important data is what you need to do. There will be many a garbage that will be available in the public domain. Be careful not be swayed by loads of useless data.

During this stage one must sift through the information's collected and stack them in groups or sections. If the project already exists, try to get the actual brief form the owners of the project. If for this purpose, Letters of Introduction is required from the Institute, please get them from the HoD or Competent Authority of your Institute.

Project brief may also be collected from the Architect, in case of a live project. Here it must be made very clear that do not even try to have a look at the Architects Concept. Start your work as if you are the first one doing the Design.

Here it also must be remembered that collect anything and everything that you think may be of use. Store this data properly for future use.

## 3.2 Development Control Rules

Along with the Project brief, the Project Site Plan and Zoning Plan along with applicable regulations are required to be collected. Every Town or City will have its Development Control Regulation (DCR) and must be collected for later use.

These may also be available in the internet in most cases. However, if the same is not available in the soft domain, hard copies may have to be purchased or arranged for. Sometimes, there are part Revisions or Modifications to such Control Guidelines or Rules. It is to be ascertained that the latest version along with all amendments are being used by you for the purpose.

## 3.3 Zoning & Planning Guidelines

In addition to the above, collecting Zoning regulations which may affect the Project site in question also has to be studied in details. It must be noted that the Jury may be aware of each and every details regarding that zone and it may be foolish to think that no one would know. Many cities have the separate Building and Town Planning Departments, and may have separate set of Rules and by-laws, which are to be obeyed.

Also, in some situations, the prescriptions laid down by these two bodies may contradict each other. To avoid this peculiar position,

Officers from the department or practicing Architects may be consulted for clarification.

Zoning and planning Regulations generally dictate the Land Use pattern and restrictions, Future Alignments of Government controlled or aided infrastructure, height restrictions etc.

## 3.4 Info on available Site services

As has been mentioned earlier, mapping of all externally available building services is required to be made and presented correctly in the introductory study sheets.

Location of Water Supply pipes, their ratings, volume inflow etc must be clearly documented.

In case of electrical supply, the Rating etc must be collected. Here it must be noted the various Electricity Distribution boards or companies have different set of regulations, that need to be followed.

## 3.5 Old References

As has been said earlier, the topics chosen may have part similarities with some old projects or dissertations. These references are required to be collected to the extent possible by visiting Library's.

Also similar projects that may have been built may also be referred to for clarity of though and expression. Old references are always handy for the purpose of study of the finer details of planning.

## 3.6 Site Information

As is well known, a project requires a Site. Thus collection of all information related to the chosen site is the most important part of the Data Collection. The information's that must be collected to the least is:

- Site map with dimensions & North Line
- Zoning plan if applicable
- Character of all adjoining buildings
- Urban Landscape
- Development Control Regulation & Bye Laws
- Special Govt. alignments/proposals
- On Site available Services
- Contour Plan, if applicable
- Climatic Conditions
- Annual Rainfall data
- Summer & Winter positions
- Sun Path of the location
- External influence parameters

Elaborate details on this issue have been made in the forthcoming chapters.

## 3.7 Site Connectivity Data

All features linked to access and connectivity to the project site should be mapped. Physical connection, like roads or highways, their width, type and nature is required to be noted. The exact nature of the Right of Way (ROW) is required to be found. If required, measurement of the same may be made. This measurement should include width of the footpaths, carriageway etc. All features abutting the plot and its adjoining area to be noted and mapped in the Project Site Plan.

It is also required to be found if any Future Road has been planned by the government or similar Local Development Statute. All information related to such future alignments may also be mapped for a realistic approach to the Project.

## 3.8 Site Topography

Mapping the site topography is very important. Getting the actual contours, if not already surveyed, may be an expensive affair and not feasible at this stage, a rough idea by visual introspection may be done. However, in case, your project has a really contoured sites, the contour map may be procured from some source.

## 3.9 Site Photos

To substantiate all the information's collected; photographs of each and every data collected may be taken. These should include plot boundary conditions, adjacent roads, service positions, and all other information's collected. It must be remembered that this documentation is very important and not a very easy task. Real skills and observation power is needed to properly represent these facts and make the Jury and others understand the real status of the site.

## 3.10 Reference Images

Collect reference images of similar buildings and study them to shape up your thoughts. Here a word of caution is important. Do not get carried away by the works of others and imitate them. Use these only to firm up your design concept an ethos. Let these images inspire you to reach a good design, which you may say is yours. Always remember what I have always said in many such forums:

## 3.11 Any other Relevant Info

Any relevant information is good in forming the brief and basic design concept. Some of the information may not be directly linked to the Thesis and Design process. But it is always a very good practice to stack all data that may be available

## 3.12 Local Climatic Conditions

Local conditions are generally taken for granted and not much care is given sometimes in the planning. Here an old saying is worth mentioning – "What is good in Hanover may not be good in Honolulu". This clearly indicates that every place has a different set of local climatic conditions and must be respected to the tee. Any disrespect will surely have an adverse effect on the architectural planning of the project. So data related to Rainfall, Sunrise and Sunset hours, prevailing wind directions during various times of the year must be clearly documented. In addition to the above, recent history of high flood levels, street inundations data etc must be collected in details.

## 3.13 Potential Study

Every city, or town or even village will have a set of published and documented DCR's. Such DCR's may or may not have revisions and exception for the Thesis Project plot. Meeting a competent Officer to collect such data is required to be done before commencement of Design, so that Development Potential and buildability can be calculated and all factors that control the development may be mapped and interpreted correctly. If such an exercise is not done, the Thesis Project may appear utopian and may be regarded in some cases as absurd.

*(*Note- Calculation of Potential has been explained in detail in my book titled 'Theory of Architecture : Concept to Commissioning')*

## 3.14 Analysis of all collected information

Till now you have been on the collection of information mode. It is time now to analyze and collate all the information collected over the previous few weeks. The data and information collected needs to be studied and tabulated and documented in the best manner to be presented in the Study Sheets. It must be remembered that all the information and data collected may not be fully useful or influence the design process. Having said that, it must be kept on record that no information or data is for the trash bins and must be ignored. One never knows how small and seemingly unimportant information may suddenly become useful during the Jury Process. It is thus suggested to have a few hidden or black out sheets where such data is stored and may be pulled up, if need be.

## 3.15 Site Analysis & Topography Study

This exercise would be very important if there are contours in the Thesis Project site. Proper Contour Study and spectrographic mapping is required to be done to understand the nature of the site. It must be remembered that a design can go awfully wrong if the site is not respected and the Design is influenced by some external event that does not have any relation with the project or project ethos. The high and low gradient zones must be clearly mapped along with high peaks and low basins.

Site sections across and along such zones must be drawn carefully to scale to understand and present site in the best possible way.

Here it is worth mentioning that the Site is your fabric for the absorbing the Dreams you have. It deserves a lot of respect.

## 3.16 Synthesis

The synthesis process must be completed with due diligence and quickly. It is not because you have less time left; it is more because that the memory process tends to die down with the passage of time. It is thus highly recommended that this process is completed fast and quick, so that any noticed gaps in information may be filled without disturbing the overall Thesis Presentation Program.

The synthesis process should try generating all the data required for preparing representative diagram using all modern methods of presentations, discussed later in this chapter. Please remember that these will become the foundations of the design about to evolve. So to make others understand the viewpoint, you must understand yourself and believe in it.

A correct and proper presentation will lead to the best understanding of the project program.

## 3.17 Collation of Data and Information

As has been discussed in the foregoing sections in the chapter, correct collation and subsequent interpretation is a very important poser. Bringing together all the data and information to a logical conclusion will be the key to the success upto this stage of work. Incorrect and inappropriate collation of data may become disastrous for the future of the Thesis Project & Dissertation.

It is here that the Thesis Guide/Mentor should play an active role and use all his experience to pave the way to correctly interpret the data and help in completing this step most effectively.

Proper collation of all data would also help organizing all the Data for quick reference and easy modification at a later date.

## 3.18 Graphical Representation

As discussed above, all the data and information that you seem to have collected must be physically studied & synthesized to make way for proper representations. Using of modern methods of representation, such as, Histograms, Pie Charts, Graphical and Pictorial Representations of data and info may be made and included in the Study Sheets.

In most cases it will be seen that there is a shortage or Information gap. It will be seen that some important data is missing, while there may be some data which is useless. The one advice that may be taken seriously over here is that DO NOT destroy or delete any information that may seem useless at this stage. Store them or dump them in a folder, so that it may be pulled up if required during the process.

## 3.19 Inference

After the tedious and tiring job of data collection is over, and the collation process is over after due analysis, the fruits of this work needs to be extracted. This is what Inference is is all about. With all the guides and restrictions in place, you will be left with an envelope to fulfill your dream. Get it right and set it on fire. The Inference from all the factors that would control your design and philosophy of design would lead you to a thought and form. Think over it. Get going

## 3.20 Final Design Opinion

From this point onwards, the design process should commence. There may be certain changes in the project program and the design brief may be reviewed based on the inputs received and data collated at a later date, if need be. For all practical purposes, there should not be any looking back on the design brief after this stage. The Final Program thus drawn must then be frozen for the future of the entire remaining Thesis preparation process.

## 3.21 Final Project Brief

Based on all the above, a tabular Project Brief must be formulated including requirements of all Indoor and Outdoor activity. The brief must contain all areas that are built and also unbuilt.

Many might think that what this unbuilt area is. To clarify, it is those areas like parking, Playgrounds etc that do not form a part of the overall Covered Area but definitely form a part of the planning brief.

Understanding the Project Brief is also very important. There may be some spaces or nomenclature which is new. Check these out and collect information that is available in the public domain. If you are not satisfied with them, take advice from your Guide or people of knowledge on the particular type of building.

***"Look at everything you see with the eyes of a REVOLUTIONARY.***

***Touch it...feel it...own it...follow it".***

# STEP 4: DESIGN INCEPTION

FIRE YOUR DREAM

# STEP 4: FIRE YOUR DREAMS

## 4.0 DESIGN INCEPTION

4.1 Relationship Matrix

4.2 Bubble Diagram

4.3 Flow Chart

4.4 Re-collation of Design Brief

4.5 Initiation of the Design Process

4.6 Development Control Rules

4.7 Natural Design Options

4.8 Blocking Options

4.9 Design Efficiency Study

4.10 Discussion with Guide & Mentors

4.11 Final Call on Concept Design Option

4.12 Roadmap & Way Forward Plan

## 4.0 DESIGN INCEPTION

It is said that 'Well begun is half done', and so true it is. To start in the best and windward direction is a matter that can be achieved with systematic approach to the entire concept. Firing the concept with the desired proportion of fuel is important. So this is the stage that makes or breaks the entire process. Be patient. Do not hurry up things and wait for the mental trigger to set the ball rolling.

### 4.1 Relationship Matrix

A great way to start a new project design is to prepare a Relationship Matrix that has the Design Brief, the Areas and the Relationship between the spaces according to their importance.

This matrix should also capture the visual models of spaces in the ascending and or descending order of all areas as per zones or space sub-divisions.

This Matrix should be carefully charted to explain the entire space to space mapping along with the Zone to Zone mapping and their respective areas.

## 4.2 Bubble Diagram

Once the Relationship Matrix is done with, a Bubble Diagram must be prepared to demonstrate the space and areas that must be near or far to each other. The Bubble Diagram must also capture spaces within spaces, and establish relationship bubbles between spaces to help finding the planning philosophy of the Project. Bubbles may overlap into each other to show that there are overlapping roles. If this is established and understood correctly, there is no chance that the Design will functionally go wrong.

## 4.3 Flow Chart

Once the Bubble Diagram is done, the Flow Chart will automatically be understood and based on the design and planning philosophy, the Flow of Action for the various faculties of the Project will be determined. Such flow will also try to highlight location and zones where there may be interference between two sets of activities or clash of flow of user or building service. The purpose of the Flow Chart is to correctly portray the various circulation paths of the project that exist between the different activities.

To elaborate on this, it may be said that a well made Flow Chart made from a correct Bubble diagram will always lead to a very measured and calculated design process and will avoid things done in a hurry or just off the hat.

## 4.4 Re-collation of Design Brief

Once the above steps are fulfilled and done with, a relook at the Design Brief and Project Program may be a very good idea. This helps in confirming the philosophy of the project parameters, and if required making small changes to the existing program. The Re-collation process must be completed in a very thoughtful manner, so that there is no thought that is left inventoried.

## 4.5 Initiation of the Design Process

To initiate a design process, the following information's are required in full:

- Project Type
- Project Program
- Project Site
- Development Control Regulations
- Design Philosophy

Once all these are ready and in hand, a small informal Inception Report can be prepared and discussed with the Thesis Guide/ Mentors and corroborated with the thoughts and ideas that have been ploughed in the process so far.

It may so happen that your thesis Guide/Mentor will recommend a few modifications in this Inception Report. Note them down and try to incorporate them to the extent feasible so that the depth of the study gets a nod from experts and the Project Inception is founded on the right pair of tracks.

## 4.6 Development Control Rules

Out of all the points that need a relook, the DCR is one of the most important one as there are many aspects that are to be followed and any deviation may be construed as a Non-complaint Design. To keep it in the proper perspective, this revisit should confirm once again that the whole inception data that has been generated till this time, is good for use in the next stage of work.

## 4.7 Natural Design Options

Based on the Inception Report, the available DCR, and the Potential Study Report mentioned earlier, a Basic Design Option may be prepared. This Initial block plan must ensure that all of the Project requirements are met with, keeping an eye on the available Building Rules.

The initial design option will be more an extension of the Bubble diagram drawn to scale as per the areas required per space. It is here when the design skills of the Architect comes in play. A good Architect will notice that the design that is evolving will flow naturally and like a jigsaw puzzle, all the blocks will fall in place.

The point to note here is that if you feel that you need to stretch and the blocks do not fit in as desired, you must imagine that the design approach may have to be changed or tweaked or thought afresh. This signal will come and must be decoded at the correct time.

Failure to understand that the concept being taken forward may be of no good use later is not desired and thus giving the necessary hawk eye look at this stage is very important. It has been observed that many a times, this stage is taken too casually.

Another very important aspect that is required to be remembered at this stage is to not bother much about the blocking or 3D view. Just follow your heart and the functional requirement of the inter-related spaces that the Flow Chart dictates and work around it as it would have suggested.

The old adage of Architecture that 'Form follows Function' should be followed to the tee. Once the basic planning, what I sometimes call the Basic Design Concept is ready, the circulation cores and other functionalities and spaces will fall generally fall in place.

## 4.8 Blocking Options

Once the above milestone is reached, various blocking options may be tried and tested. Blocking options will and should give ideas of how best the concept can be taken forward without sacrificing much on the space and relationship matrix.

If at all any or some compromises are required to be made, it should be well judged and a very decided decision must be taken. It must be remembered that the reasons for such compromise must be well grounded and kept ready for future reference if questioned later.

Also the compromise must be kept as your design secret and should be made to look like an asset in the design.

## 4.9 Design Efficiency Study

Once the design is conceptually ready, Design Efficiency Study (DES) should be conducted. DES helps us understand how efficient the design is working out and changes that may be required to be done to make the design more efficient, or in other words, more economic.

It must be remembered here that different kinds of buildings have different efficiency percentage as the best case scenario. Efficiencies are generally calculated on the basis of Overall Area is to Useable Area. This means that the circulation areas, which are also called non performing area, are checked and limited within a permissible percentage. For most kinds of buildings, DES should be within the range of 70% to 80%, unless the project is of a special type.

## 4.10 Discussion with Guide & Mentors

Once the Design Efficiency is satisfactorily achieved, one must make a check back with the Thesis Guide and other Mentors, to reconfirm and reaffirm that the design process is on the right track. While the Thesis Guide will be more of an Academician, the Mentor may be someone from the industry who has experience in the Design Type of the Thesis Project. Industry inputs are always useful and important for any good design, as it will reinforce your confidence, as the suggestions offered by the Industry Experts will be of immense value always

Care should also be taken by the Thesis Guide to ensure that the Project is run over by atleast one Architect from the Industry.

## 4.11 Final Call on Concept Design Option

After this phase is passed successfully and the design has taken all the necessary beating, a Final Call on the overall Concept Design must be taken, so that the next phase of work may commence.

Inputs taken from all sources must be understood and re-verified, and the one's which would really make the design much better may be adopted and incorporated.

## 4.12 Roadmap & Way Forward Plan

Once the Inception Report and the Design Options are ready and a go ahead is received after preliminary review from the Thesis Guide and may be Institute, a Road Map may be prepared to chalk out the next course of action.

This Road Map or Time Activity chart must find out and document on a weekly basis all the various steps required to be activated till completion, submission and Presentation.

It would be like setting milestone for the activities against a date of completion with some float so that a miss by a day or two does not raise false alarms within you.

For the final two weeks, excluding the last week, this Road Map should capture the activities on a day to day basis.

The Final week should be excluded from this program and kept as Reserve for allowing any spill over.

***"There are no fixed rules to design***

***You set your own for others to follow".***

# STEP 5: PRELIMINARY DESIGN

ADD COLOUR TO THE DREAM

# STEP 5: ADD COLOUR TO YOUR DREAM

## 5.0 PRELIMINARY DESIGN

5.1 Extension of Design Ideas

5.2 Design Development

- Structural Concept
- HVAC Concept
- Electrical Concept
- Sanitary Concept Design
- Fire Management Concept
- Acoustic Concept Design

5.3 Restructuring Bubble Diagram

5.4 Revisiting Flow Chart

5.5 3D Concepts and Modeling

5.6 Master Planning

5.7 Traffic Circulation Plan

5.8 Area Matrix

## 5.0 PRELIMINARY DESIGN

Having settled to an idea that you have nurtured, it is high time to refine it. The journey has to be taken forward, but how. Start adding the lesser important aspects of the design and initiate the thinking in a more holistic way. This is like adding colour to a black and white image to bring in more life,

### 5.1 Extension of Design Ideas

The Design idea that has been finalized has to be now taken to the next level. The Concept Design needs to be detailed out and areas worked out and matched with the design brief that has been finalized. Any tweaking that may be required in the project program has to be dealt with at this stage. It will be observed that the Concept Design when taken to the next level will suffer some bi-directional changes. While the Preliminary Design will be an extension of this thought, simultaneous changes in the Project Program will be an obvious exercise that will be required to be carried out side by side.

The Design may be required to be reviewed intensely both by the Guide and all the Mentors, if there are more than one. This review should include all possible angles of the design including 3D conceptions and blocking ideas, efficiency, DCR Compliance etc

## 5.2 Design Development

Most people often ask, as what is the role of Design Development (DD) in an Architectural Thesis Program. The answer is clear and loud. All this while up to preliminary stage, the other aspects of Architecture, that is the Engineering side is generally not thought of or is not given the space it deserves. The Preliminary Design thus is required to be developed to the next stage which is called the DD stage.

In this stage the inputs that are required to be studied and incorporated are the following:

- Structural Concept Design Inputs
- HVAC Concept Design Inputs
- Electrical Concept Design Inputs
- Sanitary Concept Design Inputs
- Fire Management Concept Design inputs
- Acoustic Concept Design Inputs

### Structural Concept

The first thing that the finalized Concept Design extended to the Preliminary Design must be put to test is the Structural System of the Design. Column Grids, Beam Locations etc must be finalized in this stage with tentative sizes. Columns then must be located and drawn in the various floor plans to identify possible clashes within the design.

All such possible clashes must be solved in the best possible way so that the design philosophy is not compromised.

### HVAC Concept

Many in the industry think that it is not the job of the Architect to think about HVAC or any such building Services. Alas, this is not true. Architects concept must capture all the aspects of Building Design and not having sufficient knowledge about building services is a definite disadvantage.

The Air-conditioning System needs to be thought of at this stage and possible duct runs decided. It must be remembered here that determination of height of a floor is dictated by the system and duct run with sizes. Thus location of AC Plant Room, external units, AHU Rooms, voids and shaft may be shown to make the design look practical and realistic.

For this, if required, professional help from the Mentor and Guide may be taken.

Another very important aspect of HVAC is Ventilation. Basements and similar spaces where ventilation is required must be addressed to demonstrate that the same has been thought of in the Design process. Ventilation Shafts and Fan Rooms etc may be shown in plan for the purpose, as and where required.

## Electrical Concept

The Electrical Design Concept is as important as others. No building can run without electricity, in some form or the other. For large sized projects where the Electrical Load may run into Mega Watts (MW), proper space planning must be done to accommodate the equipments required to be installed for the purpose.

Imagine a huge Mall or a Multi storied apartment with no Electrical Room or Electrical Substation. Will it not look unreal and immature to present a plan like this before a room full of very knowledgeable Jury!

So the best thing is to think of the Electrical Design Concept with help from others including the Mentor. Once the concept is made, as may be required, Electrical Substation with HT Room, LT Room, Switch Rooms and Electrical Rooms in various floors and zones, DG Room etc. may be shown in the Plans.

Electrical Shafts to the extent possible must also be shown in the plans as and where that may be required.

### Sanitary Concept Design

Although much may not be required to be shown with respect to Sanitary Design in an Architectural Design Thesis, Sanitary shafts, Pump Rooms and/or STP locations may b shown.

For buildings with very high plumbing interface, such as Hotels, Hospitals etc, Plumbing inputs may be shown as they form a very integral part of the overall design concept, and ignoring these may be suicidal.

### Fire Management Concept

Fire Management involves two aspect of the design concept, Protection and Detection. While detection is not very space consuming, Protection & Fighting is. To take care of this, for building designs that may fall under the Category of Fire Management as per the Building Code of the Area or Country, necessary spaces must be shown as may be required.

Fire Pump Room, Control Room etc may be shown in the Plan along with location of Wet Risers in the Staircases. Necessary Fire Shafts may also be shown to take care of these aspects.

Distance between Staircases must also be checked with the provisions of the NBC so that these are complied with in the Design

### Acoustic Concept Design

Again, buildings that may require Acoustic Engineering Inputs may require special help from the Thesis Guide or Mentor. Thesis Design topics with Cinema, Auditorium etc as elements in the Design Program may have to address a few Acoustic Engineering Issues. It may be worthwhile to show Cavity walls, Acoustic check Lobbies, Acoustic False Ceilings etc to demonstrate that the concept of Acoustics in the overall Design has been thought of.

Here it must be noted that sizing of any or all the above engineering inputs is not so important, but demonstration of the fact that these have been taken into consideration and understood properly is the key issue.

## 5.3 Restructuring Bubble Diagram

A relook at the already prepared Bubble Diagram may be a very good idea at this stage of work when the design has come to a realistic position. A check back ensures that the initial study philosophy and the concept design are on the same page and do not conflict with each other.

If at all there are a few that may appear at this stage, the same may be rationalized to bring them to order.

## 5.4 Revisiting Flow Chart

The same is also good for the Flow Chart and must be revisited together with the Bubble Diagram. It may so happen that during design process, the established flow found during case studies may be difficult to observe. In such cases, it will be very important to establish why the design flow being suggested may be better than the commonly understood norm.

It may be overtly true that there will arise contradictions between the former and later. Not to worry. This is natural.

## 5.5 3D Concepts and Modeling

This stage of work will require a booster doze to propel the design thoughts and philosophy. A look and feel of the 3D concept of the Project is the only thing that can serve this purpose.

Form does follow Function but that does not mean that Form is not important. The natural

Form generated out of a good design will always work and result in an efficient design.

As I write this book, the most commonly tool used for this method is the 'SketchUp'. There may be many other such tools and any of them may be used to understand the concept. While the 3D model is being studied and prepared, the planning may be required to be tweaked and adjusted to accommodate a certain idea in the overall form.

That is fine. No problems. Just go ahead.

Shifting of certain elements or making minor adjustments is very common and doable without regret.

Also the play of solids and voids, Light and shade must be clearly understood before concluding this stage.

## 5.6 Master Planning

All this while, we have talked about the building only. Now the building and the site will have to be thought together and an overall blend has to be made. All external spaces must be planned at this point of time including location of all Roads, Pathways Entry Gates etc. Circulation pattern of Vehicles,

Pedestrian, their segregation plan etc must be carefully solved during Master Planning.

Aesthetic elements such as Water Bodies, Fountains, and Landscaping elements must also be conceptually captured at this stage.

Needless to say that for Thesis Projects having more than one building in a site, external space planning and zoning of the Master Plan is very important and is the starting point of this process. It is important to thus first prepare a zoning plan to earmark spaces for the various functions which may or may not have inter-space relationship.

## 5.7 Traffic Circulation Plan

As has been mentioned in the foregoing paragraph, Traffic flow, entry and exits, drop off locations, parking zones, traffic lay-bye bays etc form an integral part of the Master Planning. Right from the point of entry to the exit, all possible traffic movement conditions and scenarios must be studied and addressed in the Master plan.

For projects where there may be multiple modes of transportation, all required modes may be studied to help find out the concept with least conflicts.

Parking design and planning is also a very important aspect that will be required to be addressed in the Master Plan. Surface and covered parking, as the case may demand, will have to be shown in line with the requirements of the DCR of the Area. If required Multi Level Car Parks (MLCP) may be planned to cater to the requirement of projects with high parking demands.

## 5.8 Area Matrix

The last important step before this stage is concluded is to prepare an Area Matrix and compare the same with the originally conceived Project Program. It will be seen that certain areas due to architectural limitations do not match the original provisions.

Do not get panicked. There will be ways and means to solve this if the differences are big and unrealistic. Making changes in the Design to suit is one of the better options, but may not be possible sometimes due to the pressure of massing. A compromise may be made and the study areas back calculated to make up for the change.

Also some areas, mostly the Building Services areas may not have appeared in the original program. This is very natural. Just add them at this stage and mention the same in the original space program.

***"It is all about Inner Beauty with Outer Presence."***

# STEP 6: SCHEMATIC DESIGN

ADD SOME EMOTION

# STEP 6: ADD SOME EMOTION

**6.0 SCHEMATIC DESIGN DESIGN**

6.1 Final Design

6.2 Elevation Study

6.3 Sectional Analysis

6.4 3D Concepts

6.5 Structural Design Inputs

6.6 Mechanical & Electrical Inputs

6.7 Synergy with Finalized Design

6.8 Necessary Revisions

## 6.0 SCHEMATIC DESIGN

What happens when we experience a character that portrays his role without any emotion? We call it lifeless and term it as bad acting. And yes, a design without any emotions is a bad design.

If the analogy is not understood, let me clarify. Emotion is generated out of environment, climate, feeling and many other earthly things. We often hear people talking about controlling emotions.

Now what is emotion got to do with Architecture. As I feel, a building is not only brick and mortar; door and window, floor and ceiling. It is much more. To make it habitable, we need a lot of building services discussed in the earlier chapter to supplement the functions of the building. These are things that controls the quality of life inside and out the building.

### 6.1 Final Design

This stage of the work is by all means the final lap of this mammoth task. And to bring it to its best logical conclusion, this lap has to be run with full fortitude. The motto at this stage should be Citius, Altius & Fortius.

The Final design involves many components of work which needs to be taken care in the best possible way. This stage has to bring forward the best possible output from your skill sets that have been honed for the last 5 years. The entire design now needs to be drawn keeping in mind all aspects of final presentation. Wall thickness, Doors, Windows, Openings, and Columns etc should be drawn in this stage.

## 6.2 Elevation Study

In tune with the 3D concepts, Elevations from all sides should be drawn. The elevation should try to reflect the best of the views and should not be restricted to cardinals. Necessary study to match the plans must be conducted to take a conclusive stand on this.

## 6.3 Sectional Analysis

Sectional drawings to explain all facets of the design to highlight the concept in the best possible way must be drawn. It must be remembered that Sections for the sake Sections should not be drawn. Sections must try to elaborate the niceties of the design and make understanding of the volume easier.

Changes in levels, height etc explaining all voids and the structural system should be carefully displayed and portrayed in the Sections.

## 6.4 3D Concepts

The final 3D is required to be given shape with possible finishes, foreground and background scenarios.

Draft renders should be made and matched with the planning and concept design. The 3D Model should capture the best of the design being presented.

Proper delineation of all indoor and outdoor spaces along with the play of light and shade will make the views look more interesting.

## 6.5 Structural Design Inputs

Reexamination of the structural design system with respect to columns, beams, girders trusses and roof systems must be conducted and necessary changes in the drawings must be made. The 3D model finalized must be in sync with the design being presented and wherever necessary, the Structural System should be showcased.

A basic knowledge of the structural system being proposed must be known and a few details, if possible may be presented.

## 6.6 Mechanical & Electrical Inputs

Similarly, as has been explained in the earlier chapter, all Mechanical and Electrical inputs should be once again verified so that they do not appear unrealistic in any part of the design.

The details that have been discussed in the Preliminary Design Concept stage with respect to all building services should be cross checked and reviewed under expert guidance of the Thesis Guide and or Mentor. Once these are reaffirmed, the Design can be taken as finally frozen and cast in stone.

## 6.7 Synergy with Finalized Design

Synergy with all elements of the design elements must be ensured at this stage so that there is no noticeable mismatch between concept plans, sections, elevations and 3D being presented.

If at all there is and is noticed, the same may be taken care at this stage, as there may not be any more chance to do much after this stage is crossed.

## 6.8 Necessary Revisions

Revisions, as may be required must be addressed before proceeding to the next stage. Please remember that, after this, it is all dog work and a lot of slogging will be required. The slog overs are merciless but satisfying and must be enjoyed to the fullest.

***"Your work is a live testament and timeless***

***You can never disown it."***

# STEP 7: DRAFT OUTPUT AND MOCK PRESENTATION

DRESS REHEARSAL

# STEP 7: DRESS REHEARSAL

## 7.0 DRAFT OUTPUT AND MOCK PRESENTATION

7.1 Check output for Font Sizes

7.2 Sheet Composition & Title Block

7.3 Check for Colour in Draft Output

7.4 Discuss with Guide & Mentors

7.5 Make Final Revisions

7.6 Mock Presentation

7.7 Attend Mock Jury

7.8 Note Observations made by Mock Jury

## 7.0 DRAFT OUTPUT AND MOCK PRESENTATION

This is one of the penultimate steps that may be required. Many may think that this is unnecessary and a waste of time, but believe you me, never skip this exercise. Like in a play, we have dress rehearsal, this is similar to that. Assure yourself that you are on the right path.

### 7.1 Check output for Font Sizes

A draft print of the entire submission must be taken at the appropriate scale and paper size. I personally recommend that no size bigger than A1 should be chosen for the purpose.

Once the Draft prints are ready, hierarchy of font sizes, visibility of all required information's and colour displays may be seen and studied.

It is very natural to find that some of the fonts have become too small and some rather big. Necessary checks must be done for all Texts so that they are legible and readable, as they appear.

### 7.2 Sheet Composition & Title Block

On the chosen sheet size, it is high time to compose the sheet which would hold good for the entire submission.

There are many ways to compose the sheet. Some may prefer and Bottom band design, while some other may think of a Vertical Band. The composition pattern will depend mostly on the spread of the plan and net sheet area required. According to this, the Title block composition may be finalized.

The Title block must contain certain mandatory information's as per the standards of the University or Institute. However some of the must give information's that must appear in the title block are:

- Project Name
- Sheet Content Description
- Scale of the Drawing
- North Line
- Index, if required
- Legend, if required
- Date
- Sheet Number

In addition to the above, a portion of the Title block must also be dedicated for the following:

- Name of University and/or Institute along with Logo if available
- Name

- Batch code or Details if present
- Roll Number or ID, as the case may be
- Space for Department Stamping of Hard Copy
- Any other Details as per Institute standards

## 7.3 Check for Colour in Draft Output

Since most presentations will be done in colour. It is important to check the colour print output. It must be remembered here that the Printer that will be used for taking final prints must be used for taking the Draft Prints, as the colour mix varies from printer to printer, sometimes model to model and brand to brand, thus effecting its output.

## 7.4 Discuss with Guide & Mentors

A last round of discussion must be carried out with a set of these Draft prints, and last minute suggestions taken from the Guide and Mentor. All possible inputs and observations must be addressed before taking for going ahead for the final output for presenting before the Final Grand Jury

## 7.5 Make Final Revisions

One last round of revisions may be carried out in the pertinent portions of the submission. The final revisions must address all possible presentation lacunae, such as Line thicknesses, Hatch intensities, Font sizes, Colour representations etc.

Once done with this stage, a full back up should be taken to nullify any mishap or systems crashes that may occur, touchwood, resulting in loss of data and months of hard work.

## 7.6 Mock Presentation

Every good institute arranges a Mock jury Presentation to understand the preparedness of the students concerned. These Mock Jury exercises instill confidence within the students and make them mentally prepared for the actual Jury. Such mock Jury sessions generally take place about a week before the actual date.

## 7.7 Attend Mock Jury

If such a Mock Jury is arranged by the Institute, go for it. This is like attending the Dress rehearsal of a play, where you are in the lead role. This may be done on the basis of Multi Media Projections to avoid the cost of taking Prints.

## 7.8 Note Observations made by Mock Jury

Once this mock presentation is over, the observations made by the Mock Jury may be noted and necessary changes made in the Final submission. However, any revision at this stage must be carried out with the full consent of the Thesis Guide and/or Mentor to avoid any last minute misunderstanding.

***"Your Dream is your Problem. Live up to it."***

# STEP 8: THESIS PROJECT REPORT

GET THE SCRIPT RIGHT

# STEP 8: GET THE SCRIPT RIGHT

**8.0 THESIS PROJECT REPORT**

8.1 Contents of the Project Report

8.2 Cover Section

8.3 Main Report

a. Project Background
b. Project Program
c. Goals and Objectives
d. Case Study
e. Space & Area Matrix
f. Zoning & Master Planning
g. Potential Study
h. Design Concept Note
i. Area Matrix
j. Special Remarks
k. Illustrations
l. Engineering Inputs
m. Conclusion

8.4 Annexure

8.5 Drawings

## 8.0 THESIS PROJECT REPORT

Report Writing for Architectural Thesis or Dissertation, whatever name it is called is a very important part of the entire submission. It is here where you can document all the thought, explanations, notes and remarks. It must be remembered that you may not get all the time and chance to explain your whole story in front of the Grand Jury Members within the limited allotted time. This chapter would try to give an in-depth measure of what information should be included in a Report of this importance.

### 8.1 Contents of the Project Report

The Project Report should ideally contain the following 4 sections:

- Cover Section
- Main Report
- Annexure
- Drawings

In addition to the above, some Institutes require a pocket either in front or in the back, to hold a CD or DVD where a copy of the entire submission is required to be copied in a non-editable format.

## 8.2 Cover Section

The Cover Section includes all of the introductory parts of the Report. This section ideally should contain the following pages and information:

- Front Cover- mentioning the Project title, Student Name and other Profile details such as ID, Year, batch etc; and name of Institute/University, This may be in hard cover, bound as per standard practice of the Institute.
- Inside Cover - with the same set of information
- Certificate of Submission - Grand Jury & Institute acceptance page where there is space for all the Grand Jury Members and the HoD to place their signature and Institute Seal with Date of Acceptance. This is also called Certificate of Acceptance in some Schools. (See Samples given later in this section)
- Certificate of Declaration – This is a kind of undertaking given by the student as a part of the mandatory requirement for submission of a Thesis under the B. Arch program. (See Samples given later in this section)
- Acknowledgement – This page should ideally contain all the names you would

like to thank and acknowledge their help and contribution in your journey towards the completion of your Thesis. (See Samples given later in this section)

- Bibliography – All references taken from accepted sources should be mentioned here
- Contents – To contain chapter wise head and sub heads along with Page numbers

However, it is always good to know from your institute, if there are any more Mandatory Pages or Information, that are to be inserted as per the Standard Practice & Procedure of the Institute.

A synopsis of the entire project may also be given before the Main Report. This is nothing but a kind of executive summary of the Porject.

## 8.3 Main Report

This is where all the skill is required to be demonstrated. This section should capture generally the following informations. Here it must be mentioned that the list stated below is very generic in nature. For any special type of Project, additional sections and sub-heads may have to be added.

a. ***Project Background***

The project coordinates; history and relevance should be essayed here highlighting the essence of the project and its importance. This section may also include why the chosen project is so dear to your heart and reasons for choosing the project you have chosen.

b. ***Project Program***

The Project Program should list and highlight all the spatial and non-spatial facilities that are to be provided in the Project. The Program must also include Site Details, Project Brief as conceived during the start of the Project and basic Components of the design.

c. ***Goals and Objectives***

This section should try to mention what the project would achieve and why this project. Every Project would have an objective which would try to outline the social and other impacts caused by the presence of the project. It may be prudent here to mention any published objective that the promoters of the project may have, and how this has been dealt with.

### d. *Case Study*

All details collected during the case study including reference Images and data collected must be documented here. Report on the collected data and inference drawn from the Case study must be mentioned here.

### e. *Space & Area Matrix*

Directly as an inference, the space and Area matrix should be tabulated. Along with the tabulated Spatial Brief the following must also be captured under this section.

- Bubble Diagram
- Relationship Matrix
- Flow Chart
- Analysis of the Space matrix

The Space and Area May include Pie Charts and histograms to explain how the larger and smaller areas co-exist with each other; how the more important and less important spaces talk to each other; how vertical and horizontal spaces are connected to each other.

The backbone of your design lies in how good this section is understood and presented. So one needs to be very careful with what amount of information should be included in this section.

f. ***Zoning & Master Planning***

Assuming the Thesis Project is of sizeable dimension with a Master Plan that has more than one Building or Space, a Master Plan study is required to be done.

The first job is to be categorize the various Project elements that are required to be placed in a zone. Master Plan Zoning should try to bring forward the Spatial Occupancy of the various Elements that would capture each zone along with their connections, internal and external.

g. ***Potential Study***

To start with this section, a complete Study of the Local Building Regulations and Development Control Rules (DCR) must be analyzed and synthesized along with prescriptions that are to be followed with respect to the National Building Code (NBC).

Subsequent to this, a diagrammatic Potential Study needs to be done to find out and explain how the planning concepts have been arrived at. As this study plays a very important part in the formation of the Initial Concept Design, no mistake or oversight should be allowed.

(for details of how to conduct Potential Study, my book – *Theory of Architecture: Concept to Commissioning* may be referred)

### h. *Design Concept Note*

The Design Concept Note should ideally cover the Design Philosophy and inspirations that have led to the particular the design. A detail commentary on the location of the various facilities along with relevance should be made in this section.

The Concept note should generally cover the following:

- Design Elements
- Inter Relationship of spaces and how they have been dealt with
- Design Philosophy
- Inspirations
- Circulation, both Horizontal & Vertical
- Efficiency of design
- Design highlights

- Structural Challenges
- Mech. & Electrical Engg. Systems
- External Spaces
- Roads and Pathways
- Parking
- Landscaping

### i. *Area Matrix*

A detailed Area Statement showing all Area and Spaces in a tabular form must be presented. This table must be prepared section wise with two possible columns 'Required" and 'Proposed'. Also compliance with Local statutory regulations must be highlight in this section. Notwithstanding anything, the table should capture the fcat that the proposed design has been conceived within the framework of all Rules & Regulations, Statutes and effective Codes of practice.

### j. *Special Remarks*

Any special Remark on the Design should be made here. This section may contain Environmental issues, societal issue, Socio-Cultural issues and many more. If there are points to make that the design has been conceived from any particular theme, that may also be mentioned here, with reference to the submitted Design.

### k. *Illustrations*

Self Made hand sketches and images in support of the Design Commentary may be included in this section and how the design has been influenced by them. It may be better to scan the original concept sketches and show how the concept has been developed from the given project program.

These sketches will truck in all the thoughts that have been injected in the concept, while the design process was on and going.

### l. *Engineering Inputs*

The Mechanical and Electrical inputs that have been used and integrated with the design must be captured here. The items that may be included in this section should cover all the possible Building Services Interface along with Structural System Design

- Structural Design Inputs
- HVAC Concept Design Inputs
- Electrical Concept Design Inputs

- Sanitary Concept Design Inputs
- Fire Management Concept Design inputs
- Acoustic Concept Design Inputs

A detail Concept Note on all of the above items, as may be applicable may be talked about in this section. Here it must be remembered that only the concept should be discussed here and no calculations should be included.

### m. Conclusion

A concluding section must be written to sum up entire design fabric and Note. The Conclusion should not be too long and must be very compact and concise.

## 8.4 Annexure

This Section should contain all reference Plates, build up Drawings, Photographs and all images or data that have been referred to in various parts of the Report. It is a good practice to index this entire Section and sequence them in a particular order.

## 8.5 Drawings

A full set of drawings submitted along with a list of drawings may be included. The Drawings should be printed fit to sheet size of the Report, so that these drawings can act as a ready reckoner and easy reference.

## 8.6 Samples of Cover Section submission

As mentioned in Section 8.2, most Universities/ Institutions require the following to be a part of the Thesis Report submission . The text given herein after is just a sample followed and needs to be verified from the Institute. The exact protocol and standards that are to be followed must be checked with the Institute's concerned office.

***"Go back to Nature for all your Answers***

***You will never be disappointed."***

## CERTIFICATE OF DECLARATION

This is to state that he Architectural Thesis titled 'Name of Project' has been carried out by the undersigned is in partial fulfillment of the requirement for award of Degree in Bachelor of Architecture at The "*Name of Institute*" and/or University under the Supervision and Guidance of "Name/s of Thesis Guide"

The undersigned hereby declares that the matter embodied in the Thesis is original and has not been submitted to any other Institution for any Degree, Diploma or similar title

---------------------------

Name of Student

ID Number

Date: dd-mmm-yyyy

## CERTIFIACTE OF ACCEPTANCE

This is to certify that he Architectural Thesis titled '*NAME OF PROJECT*' has been submitted by "*NAME OF STUDENT*", final year student of Architecture, Semester – X, from ........(Month & year)8 to ......(month & year) to the undersigned.

On successful completion of the Bachelor of Architecture Degree Course by the candidate, the undersigned hereby accepts the Thesis Report along with all its enclosures on behalf of the School of Architecture, so that the same may be placed in the Architectural Library for future use and record.

---------------------------------- ---------------------------------------

Name of Student
ID Number
Date
Place

Principal or HoD(as the case may be)
Name of Institute
Name of University
Place

## ACKNOWLEDGEMENT

Writing an Acknowledgement is no mean task. However, this is a task that needs to be done.

With all humility, I would like to take this opportunity to express my deepest gratitude to .............. (mention name of *Mentor/Thesis Guide) for all the help and guidance given to me and acting as a Mentor to our work. He has been the pillar of our strength and the motivation behind me to become what I am today. That you Sir/Madam, for showing us the light, and helping us complete this wonderful journey, which started five years ago. I would remain ever indebted for the patient and critical guidance given throughout this great journey, even sometimes at odd hours, to complete this Thesis in an unique manner and make the journey so interestingly beautiful.

I would also remain grateful to my **Thesis Guide ........... (mention name, Designation, Institute name) for helping me during this journey.(if Guide & Mentor are different persons)

I am also obliged to ................................, and ................................ (mention all names and positions of all the Faculty names) for the immense help and constructive criticism offered during the process.

I most respectfully extend my gratitude towards Prof.................................., (mention name etc, HoD or Principal or Head) for being there with us.

I would also acknowledge the help that was extended by the following individuals to shape up this Thesis:

1. ........................................

2. ........................................

(Mention all the names & designation from whom help has been taken, basically external, like from the Industry etc)

Last but not the least; I would fail in my duty if I did not acknowledge the immense help offered to me by my friends and well-wishers. A special mention is due here to my Junior Brothers and Sisters for the active support and the sleepless nights they spent to see this day of my successful completion. No word is big enough to express this gratitude.

This Architectural Thesis has been carried out with the help of many individual. Among them I have tried to mention a few names by way of special acknowledgement. Any involuntary error or omission is deeply regretted and is unintentional.

*Note :* ** Mention name of the person who has been of maximum help. It could be any person inside or outside the Institute*
*** If the above person is not your thesis Guide, mention here his name. Or else delete this paragraph.*

*Remark: The above may be edited and only required portions given.*

# STEP 9: FINAL PRESENTATION

THE STAGE IS SET

# STEP 9: THE STAGE IS SET

## 9.0 FINAL PRESENTATION

9.1 Selection of Final output Medium & Paper Size

9.2 Final Drafting

9.3 3D Modeling Fine Tuning

9.4 3D Image Extracts from Final Design Model

9.5 Take Final Prints in Suitable Media

9.6 Check for clarity again

9.7 Thesis Report

9.8 Back Up & Make distributable Soft Copy

# 9.0 FINAL PRESENTATION

## 9.1 Selection of Final output Medium & Paper Size

Once the final lot of drawings is ready, the medium of presentation must be fixed. The paper size of the output along with scale must be selected and draft outputs may be studied. If the paper size is A1, control of lone thicknesses, font sizes etc must be examined.

A sequence of presentation of display material may be fixed so that the flow during the final presentation may be in line with the concept design.

## 9.2 Final Drafting

For all practical purposes, it will be seen that there are few mismatches in the draft output. Colour and line properties are some of the most common items that require a final review. Also it is important to study the intensities of Hatches that may have been done in the rendering and material assignment in drafting.

Once this is done, the process may be repeated until a satisfactory result is obtained.

## 9.3 3D Modeling Fine Tuning

A similar exercise must be done with the 3D views that will be presented. Here it must be clarified that all fine tuning must be done to come to the logical conclusion of the design process.

## 9.4 3D Image Extracts – Final Design Model

Once this stage is arrived, Image extracts may be done for rendering and final presentation. As this may involve cross platform rendering, the final product must be examined with a very big magnifier. Any defect or mismatch may be addressed and taken care at this stage.

## 9.5 Take Final Prints in Suitable Media

The Final submission is now ready for grabs. Take Final Prints in best mode and try to keep the drawings flat. Please note that rolling the drawings may create cracks and scratches in the output. The prints must be preserved for the D-day after being satisfied with the quality of the output.

## 9.6 Check for clarity again

If it is found that any drawing has a lack of clarity or does not give the desired effects, reprints of the same may be taken after make necessary corrections to cancel out the defects.

## 9.7 Thesis Report

The Thesis or Dissertation Report as may be called in different institutes must be printed. The best possible size for such Report is A4 and the Landscape mode is the most acceptable orientation.

A set of drawings in A4 size may also be appended in this Report along with Area Matrix.

Number of copies that are required would be depend on the requirements of each institute and must be checked with the competent Authority for information on the same.

## 9.8 Back Up & Make distributable Soft Copy

Once all is ready and right, a back u[p of all stage of work should be taken in the editable format of work. This will help in a long way to restore lost data if, for any reason, something is lost.

Along with this a full set of pdf of the Final product must be made for distribution, if required by the Institute. These may be stored or copied in CD's or DVD's for the purpose with proper identification such as Name. Year, ID etc along with Project title

***"The Architect is the captain of the ship.***

***If you cannot steer it, someone else will."***

# STEP 10: GETTING READY

PULL THE CURTAINS UP

# STEP 10: PULL THE CURTAINS UP

## 10.0 GETTING READY

10.1 Physical Model by self or Agency

10.2 Notes for Presentation

10.3 Keep ready all DD works

10.4 Try to Document the journey to this Design

10.5 Take note of assigned time and Serial

10.6 Keep nerves in tact

10.7 Keep Composure

## 10.0 GETTING READY

### 10.1 Physical Model by self or Agency

Some Institutes require submission of Physical Models in appropriate size and scale. If the same is mandatory or optional, as the case may be, preparatory works for preparation of the Model is required to be carried out.

If any agency has been entrusted with the work of making this Model, sufficient time must be given to the Agency for properly and correctly completing the work. It must be noted that a different set of data including a few details, surface development patterns and layouts may have to be supplied to the Agency for the purpose.

If, for any reason, the Model is to be prepared by oneself, action on this must be taken much before and suitable medium for the same must be ready for preparation of the same. Help from Juniors may also be taken for this purpose so that some help is found in these crunch hours.

### 10.2 Notes for Presentation

A small note regarding the sequence of presentation and points to be made should be prepared beforehand. The hand note or pocket note should contain all relevant data and statistics that the Jury may ask for.

One may not find time or opportunity to search for info or data.

## 10.3 Keep ready all DD works

Chronologically arrange all the works that have been done, right from day One. Do not delete any file or Folder. However, if some data or file may seem unnecessary, the same may be stored in a folder called 'Dump'

## 10.4 Try to Document the journey to this Design

It may be worthwhile to document the journey of the design process. All necessary soft and hard material may be arranged in a proper way so that the story can be told and displayed if need be.

*"Every Dream has a story. Give it Life and Enjoy"*

## 10.5 Take note of assigned time and Serial

Note down the assigned time and date of the presentation session that has been allotted to you. It may be possible that the event is taking place on multiple days. So be careful and note the slot assigned.

Also the time span allotted for each presentation must be noted.

## 10.6 Keep nerves in tact

Most people feel very nervous during this phase. It is important to keep nerves intact and keep the mind free from all encumbrances. Don't show your project submission to anyone or ask for any comment or observation from anyone. Do not allow over enthusiast to influence you at this stage.

## 10.7 Keep Composure

Do not get baulked down by any side talk or small talk about the Thesis Jury from Class Mates. Keep your composure and do not vent any idea to others. Try to sleep well and avoid losing confidence.

Get up early on the d Day and reach the Institute well before the appointed time and wait for your turn.

***"If you are not a saint.***

***Try to be one.***

***It shows in your design"***

# STEP 11: THE FINAL SHOW

LIGHTS CAMERA ACTION

# STEP 11: LIGHTS CAMERA ACTION

## 11.0 THE FINAL SHOW

11.1 Take help to Display presentation

11.2 Check Sequence of Display

11.3 Soft Version Display

11.4 Keep your Note Sheet Ready

11.5 Greet the Jury Members

11.6 Great others present

11.7 Start your presentation

11.8 Avoid politely being interrupted

11.9 Take questions when finished

11.10 Do not show Discomfort

11.11 Be Smart but not Over Smart

11.12 Accept Mistakes

11.13 Ask for answers or solutions

11.14 Thank everyone including Guide

## 11.0 THE FINAL SHOW

Yes, this is the appointed time you have been waiting for the last so many years. Use it to the best of your ability. Make it your day, so that you never would need to repent later. This is your day

### 11.1 Take help to Display presentation

Before the appointed time, display the drawings in the space provided. The sequence of display must be checked carefully. If required, help from juniors may be taken to effectively fix the display on the assigned space.

### 11.2 Check Sequence of Display

Cross check the sequence of the display once again once again before declaring readiness to face Jury.

### 11.3 Soft Version Display

If the presentation is required to be done over a Projection System, a test run may be done to ensure proper disposition and display.

Also make sure that the presentation starts from the first slide.

## 11.4 Keep your Note Sheet Ready

Once again have a good look at the Note sheet and keep it within easy reach, so that it may be referred to quickly.

Also don't forget to switch off your Mobile Phone before entering the scene of action.

## 11.5 Greet the Jury Members

At the appointed time, present yourself before the Jury Members. Introduce yourself and greet the Jury Members by a soft Good Morning or Good afternoon as relevant during the time of the day. Do not try to be overly smart and try to be modest and open to listening.

## 11.6 Greet others present

Also greet all others present including all Faculty Members and Thesis Guide Present. There may be a few who are not known. Greet them as well.

## 11.7 Start your presentation

Start your presentation from the beginning and let it flow as per the desired pattern. Try to play the game in measured speed and never try to make the Jury feel that you are in a hurry. Go step by step and don't let your flow be disturbed

## 11.8 Avoid politely being interrupted

There may be some Jury Member who may try to interrupt your method of presentation and disturb the flow. Avoid being interrupted politely and state that you will address all concerns and observations once the basic presentation is completed.

Keep a mental note of all questions.

## 11.9 Take questions when finished

After you have finished the first round of presentation, invite questions from the Member of the Jury. Start with the Jury Member who interrupted you before so that he feels comfortable.

## 11.10 Do not show Discomfort

It must be remembered that the jury is here to ask questions. Sometimes, some of the question may not be good and encouraging. If a question is uncomfortable, try to understand the question and try to give a suitable answer. The Jury may not be happy or convinced with your reply. Do not get irritated. Do not argue.

## 11.11 Be Smart but not Over Smart

Try not to be over smart and show a 'know all' attitude. Do not display or show signs of being disturbed by any question. However trying to be over smart and riding over a question may be suicidal and should be avoided.

## 11.12Accept Mistakes

It may so happen that a member of the Jury find a mistake or gives an opinion to which you may not agree. Do not get perturbed. Accept the mistake or suggestion and move ahead instead of trying to convince the jury that you were right. There will be no gain out of this and should be consciously avoided. Sometimes this may act as a self dug trap and may be difficult to come out, once in it. So it is always advisable to avoid such confrontations.

## 11.13 Ask for answers or solutions

Whenever a situation like the above occurs and you are commented, you may ask for possible answers or solutions. But one must be very careful in doing this and should not appear that you are challenging the decision for a reply. It is important to plead ignorance and politely request for upgrading your knowledge for a possible solution.

## 11.14Thank everyone including Guide

Wait for the session to end. Take permission to end and invite question to ensure that the session has really ended. If there are no more comments from anyone, with permission from the Jury close your presentation. Before ending and walking out, do not forget to thank all the members of the Jury and everyone present. Ensure to mention that it has been a wonderful and educating.

Hope this helps you.

GOD BLESS & GOOD LUCK

***"A line is not only a line in Architecture***

***It is a part of a Dream.***

***A dream nurtured by the interplay of***

***Solids and Voids, Light and Shade,***

***Colour and Texture, Foreground and Background,***

***Against a canvas called NATURE"***